UNLEASHING THE POWER OF DAILY JOY

UNLEASHING THE POWER OF DAILY JOY

There was once a time in my life when the days seemed to blur together, and I found myself eagerly awaiting the arrival of Friday. It was as if Monday through Thursday were placeholders, merely existing in a world that lacked the true happiness I craved. But when Friday arrived, a surge of excitement washed over me, signaling the arrival of the coveted weekend.

However, as I navigated my way through my thirties, a question began to haunt me: Is this truly the life I want to live? I cherished my Saturdays and Sundays, relishing the freedom they brought. I came to the realization that I had unintentionally fallen into a pattern of only looking forward to the weekends, ignoring the possibility of finding happiness during the other days of the week.

I realized it was time for a change. I embarked on a journey of self-reflection and transformation, with a strong resolve to break free from the limitations of my own mindset. I began to take charge of my thoughts to reshape my reality. I refused to simply watch from the sidelines as life passed me by.

This book is a testament to the power of embracing a different perspective—one that embraces the beauty and possibility of every single day. It chronicles my journey of breaking free from the clutches of living for Fridays and discovering the abundance that exists in the present moment.

UNLEASHING THE POWER OF DAILY JOY

Through these pages, we will explore the profound mindset shifts, the cultivation of gratitude, and the pursuit of purpose that allowed me to escape the Monday-through-Friday monotony. Through practical insights, heartfelt reflections, and actionable steps, I hope to empower you to embark on your journey toward finding joy every single day.

I pray this book is a beacon of hope, shedding light on the endless opportunities that come with cherishing every moment and realizing that happiness is not limited to a particular day of the week. Together, let us forge a path towards a life that is deeply fulfilling, where every day becomes an opportunity for joy, growth, and true contentment.

With heartfelt wishes,

Justyn

UNLEASHING THE POWER OF DAILY JOY

CONTENTS

UNLEASHING THE POWER OF DAILY JOY

CONTENTS

DRINK THE COFFEE

As we begin each day, it's easy to get caught up in the hustle and bustle of our lives and forget to take a moment for ourselves.

But stop...

Take a few minutes every morning to do something that brings you joy. God wants us to experience joy in our lives, and finding pleasure in the simple things is one way to do that. Taking care of our well-being enables us to better serve both God and those around us throughout the day. When we take the time to prioritize our happiness each day, we are also strengthening our relationship with God.

So take a few moments each morning to do something that brings you joy. It could be reading a book, practicing yoga, or simply enjoying a cup of coffee. Whatever it is, do it with a grateful heart and an attitude of thankfulness. Remember that true happiness comes from God, and by focusing on Him first thing in the morning, we can set the tone for a joy-filled day ahead.

Ecclesiastes 5:19 says, "Moreover, when God gives someone wealth and possessions, and the ability to enjoy them, to accept their lot and be happy in their toil—this is a gift from God." This verse reminds us that the ability to enjoy the simple pleasures in life is a gift from God. We are called to find joy in our work and the blessings God has given us and be content with what we have. Start each day with a heart full of gratitude and a commitment to seek joy in all things.

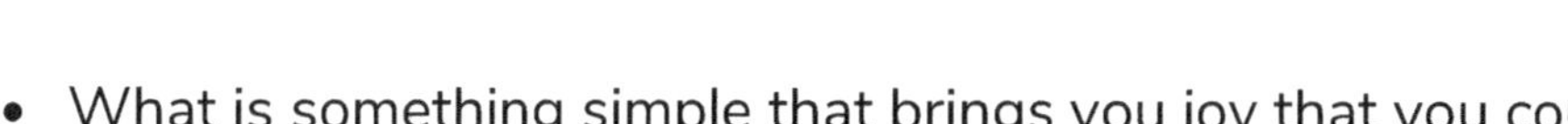

- What is something simple that brings you joy that you could incorporate into your morning routine?

MAKE THE CHANGE

Do you find yourself waking up every morning to go to a job that doesn't bring you any joy? I certainly have experienced this at times in my life! However, life is a precious gift, and it is far too short to spend most of our waking hours in a job we dislike. Deciding to quit a job can be a difficult and scary one. We may feel uncertain about the future and worry about how we will support ourselves and our families. However, sometimes leaving a job that is causing us stress or unhappiness is the best thing we can do for our mental and emotional well-being.

As we strive for happiness, it's important to acknowledge that job-related stress, anxiety, and unhappiness can have a significant impact on our overall well-being. Leaving a job that erodes our happiness is not an act of recklessness; it is an act of self-preservation and self-respect. It affirms our worth, acknowledging that our time and energy are precious. The courage to step away from a toxic job opens doors to new possibilities, allowing us to explore passions and create a life built on purpose and fulfillment.

We are encouraged to seek wisdom and discernment when making decisions. Proverbs 2:6-7 says, "For the Lord gives wisdom; from his mouth come knowledge and understanding; he stores up sound wisdom for the upright; he is a shield to those who walk in integrity." By seeking God's guidance, we can trust He will give us the wisdom to make the right choice. While the road ahead may appear uncertain, it also presents opportunities for growth, reinvention, and the pursuit of meaningful work.

MAKE THE CHANGE

If you are considering making a life change, pray and seek God's guidance. Ask Him to give you wisdom and discernment, and trust that He will provide for you as you take steps to care for your mental and emotional well-being. Philippians 4:19 reminds us, "My God will supply every need of yours according to his riches in glory in Christ Jesus." When we trust in God's provision and seek His will, we can have peace knowing He is in control.

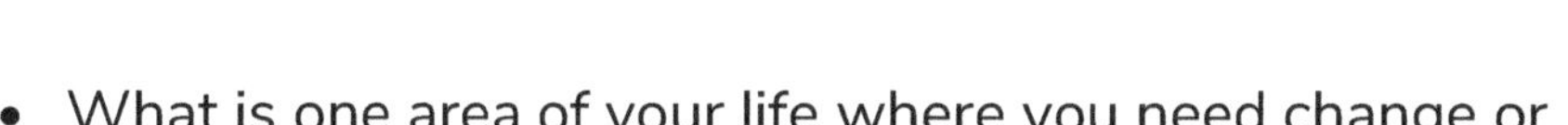

- What is one area of your life where you need change or growth? How can you take the first step toward making that change?
- Are you currently in a job or situation that is causing you stress, anxiety, or unhappiness? How can you trust in God's provision and have faith that He will provide for your needs as you take steps to care for your well-being?

LOVE WINS

Are there times when you hesitate to turn on the news or look at social media because it often leaves you feeling sad or discouraged? In our ever-changing world, polarization seems to be on the rise, and it's difficult to escape reminders of division and challenges. It's easy to lose sight of love's power in a divided and chaotic world. Yet throughout the Bible, we are reminded that love is ultimately what will overcome all obstacles and triumph over evil.

When we encounter difficult people or situations, it can be easy to allow negativity and frustration to consume us. However, as followers of Christ, we are called to respond differently. We are called to love and show kindness even when it's difficult, and to maintain an attitude of grace and forgiveness. In moments when the world brings sadness or worry, we can turn to God for comfort and hope. We can seek His wisdom and guidance when responding to our challenges. We can pray for those affected by the difficulties and look for ways to bring positive change and make a difference in the world.

Philippians 4:8 states, "Finally, brothers and sisters, whatever is true, whatever is noble, whatever is right, whatever is pure, whatever is lovely, whatever is admirable—if anything is excellent or praiseworthy—think about such things." This verse reminds us that finding joy in the midst of difficult people or distressing news begins with a shift in perspective. It involves focusing on the things that are good, true, and praiseworthy.

Joy is not dependent on external factors or the behavior of others. True joy is a deep-rooted, internal state of being that comes from our relationship with God and our perspective on life. It is a gift that God offers to us regardless of the difficulties we encounter. It's important to search for the positive aspects of individuals and hope for the strength to overcome difficult situations through prayer. You can find strength and peace that transcends your circumstances through prayer and surrendering your burdens to God.

- How can you choose joy and respond with love and grace when dealing with difficult people or encountering bad news?
- How can you demonstrate patience, kindness, and forgiveness to those around you?

EVERYTHING DOES NOT NEED A RESPONSE

In today's world of instant communication and social media, it can be easy to feel pressure to respond to every message, email, or notification that comes our way. We may feel like we must constantly be available and responsive, even if it means sacrificing our time, energy, and mental well-being.

Yet...everything does not need a response!

In fact, there are times when it may be better to refrain from responding, especially if doing so would only add fuel to the fire or cause unnecessary stress and anxiety. There was a time in my life when I always felt the need to get the last word in or give my opinion. But over time, I realized that most people don't need my opinion. Oftentimes they just need me to listen. We might overanalyze the situation and think that since everyone else is responding that certainly, we need to respond too. Nonetheless, our lack of action and silence can still be considered a form of response. You are responding by determining that a response is unnecessary and respecting the fact that not everything has to do with you or requires your attention.

In 1st Kings 5:12, the Lord gave Solomon wisdom, and Solomon wrote the whole book of Proverbs. God is no respecter of persons, so just as he gave Solomon wisdom, He gives all His children wisdom as we seek and meditate upon his word.

EVERYTHING DOES NOT NEED A RESPONSE

Proverbs 17:27-28 says, "The one who has knowledge uses words with restraint, and whoever has understanding is even-tempered. Even fools are thought wise if they keep silent and discerning if they hold their tongues." This passage reminds us that sometimes, the wisest course of action is to keep silent and refrain from speaking, especially if we are unsure what to say or how to respond.

Go to God and seek his wisdom before immediately offering your opinion, reaction, or words to someone. Remember--sometimes silence speaks when words cannot. There is a time for everything in life: a time to speak and a time to listen. The less you respond to things that don't deserve a response, the more peaceful your life will be.

- In what ways do you feel pressure to respond to everything, whether it be messages, notifications, or other demands on your time and attention?
- How can you prioritize your own well-being and mental health by setting boundaries and choosing not to respond to everything?

THE POWER OF WORDS

Words are powerful. They have the ability to build up or tear down. During my time as a teacher, I frequently encountered colleagues who possessed a pessimistic outlook on the students we taught. Little did I realize that the seeds of their pessimism were gradually taking root within me. Thoughts and feelings of negativity became embedded in my consciousness and began to shape my emotions toward my students. My teaching career felt overshadowed by a dark cloud, which affected my daily interactions with my students.

In hindsight, I realized my focus on the negative aspects of my profession created a culture that left me dissatisfied. By focusing on the challenges and shortcomings, I inadvertently closed myself off to the beauty and potential for growth that teaching inherently held. I found myself in a self-fulfilling prophecy, where my negative mindset influenced my experiences, creating a cycle of negativity in my teaching career.

Upon realizing this, I embarked on a journey of self-reflection and transformation. It became evident to me how significant our thoughts are in shaping our life experiences. I realized that by focusing on positivity, gratitude, and a growth mindset, I could cultivate an enthusiastic classroom culture. It was a conscious effort to reframe my perspective to see challenges as opportunities.

Proverbs 18:21 says, "The tongue has the power of life and death, and those who love it will eat its fruit." Our words have the power to shape our lives and the lives of those around us. In James 3:5-6, the tongue is compared to a small flame that can set a forest on fire.

THE POWER OF WORDS

Just as a small spark can ignite a raging wildfire, our words can ignite conflicts, cause division, and spread negativity. On the other hand, when we speak words of kindness, encouragement, and love, we can bring healing, reconciliation, and joy. Being mindful of our language is crucial, as it can be a powerful tool to inspire and encourage those around us. Each day we should strive to use our words to uplift and motivate others and make a positive impact.

The words we speak to ourselves are also important. It can be easy to speak negative words to ourselves and to focus on our weaknesses and shortcomings. However, Psalm 139:14 reminds us that we are fearfully and wonderfully made and that we are loved and valued by him. We can experience greater self-worth and confidence when we speak positive, affirming words to ourselves.

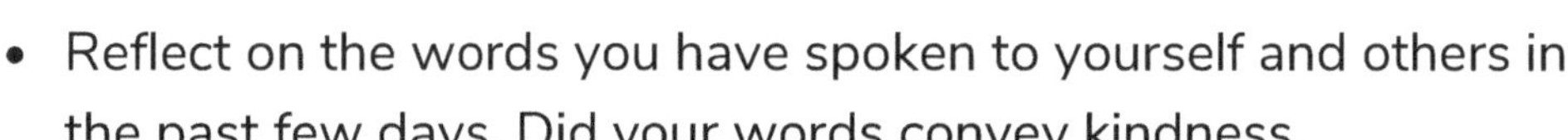

- Reflect on the words you have spoken to yourself and others in the past few days. Did your words convey kindness, encouragement, and love, or did they spread negativity?
- How can you use your words to build up others and point them toward God?

EMBRACE THE PRESENT MOMENT

Certain moments in life act as wake-up calls, prompting us to reflect on our priorities. This happened to me when I was playing with my son when he was only four years old. As he called me to look at a Lego car he had created, I found myself preoccupied with my phone. Oblivious to the impact of my divided attention, I halfheartedly glanced in his direction, pretending to be present.

Children have a remarkable intuition and an uncanny ability to detect when our attention drifts. In that fleeting instant, my child seized my hand, his tiny fingers grasping mine with determination. "MOM," he implored, his voice filled with innocence and longing, "You are not looking at me. You are looking at your phone!" In that piercing moment of truth, I realized the gravity of my actions or, rather, my lack of presence.

My son saw through me, recognizing that my mind and heart were elsewhere. It was a powerful realization of the importance of being fully present and wholeheartedly devoting my time to those I loved. In that tender interaction, I made a vow to myself to rediscover the joy of undivided connection and genuine presence with others.

Psalm 46:10 reminds us, "Be still, and know that I am God." This scripture serves as a gentle reminder to quiet the distractions and busyness of life, to be still in the moment, and to acknowledge the presence of God. By cultivating a sense of stillness and awareness, we can deepen our connections with others and fully appreciate the blessings that surround us.

EMBRACE THE PRESENT MOMENT

Have you found yourself entangled in distractions recently? Have you unintentionally missed out on precious moments with your loved ones – whether it's your child, parent, spouse, or friend – because you were too absorbed by the demands of your phone, work, or the busyness of life?

Let this be a gentle reminder to pause, breathe, and be fully present in the moments that matter most. Embrace the here and now, cherish the laughter, and create memories that will last a lifetime. Take a step back from the distractions, and wholeheartedly engage with the people and experiences surrounding you. Make a conscious effort to embrace the present moment and watch how the beauty of life unfolds before your eyes. In doing so, you'll discover a deeper sense of joy and fulfillment.

* How can you cultivate a deeper sense of presence and connection in your relationships and daily interactions?"

In today's society, we often believe that accumulating possessions will bring us happiness. We assume we need the latest gadgets, the newest clothes, and the biggest homes to be happy and successful. But the truth is, all of this excess can cause more stress and anxiety in our lives. Although there's nothing inherently wrong with having possessions, it's important to be aware of how they might divert our attention from more significant things. When we focus too much on accumulating things, we may miss out on the relationships, experiences, and moments that truly matter.

Simplifying our lives can help us to focus on what's truly important. It can help us reduce stress and anxiety and live more intentionally and purposefully. This might mean letting go of possessions that no longer serve us, creating more time in our schedules for rest and relationships, or prioritizing experiences over material goods. A few years ago, I started practicing this by giving our children trips or experiences rather than just giving them material gifts for special occasions.

Jesus tells us in Matthew 6:19-21, "Do not store up for yourselves treasures on earth, where moth and rust destroy, and where thieves break in and steal. But store up for yourselves treasures in heaven, where moth and rust do not destroy, and where thieves do not break in and steal. For where your treasure is, there your heart will be also." As we simplify our lives, we can create space to draw closer to God and focus on His plan for our lives.

SIMPLIFY YOUR LIFE

We can store treasures in heaven rather than solely focusing on the things of this world. Simplifying our lives isn't always easy, but it can lead to a more peaceful and fulfilling life. Our main priority should be to concentrate on what truly matters. Take some time to reflect on your life and consider what areas you could simplify.

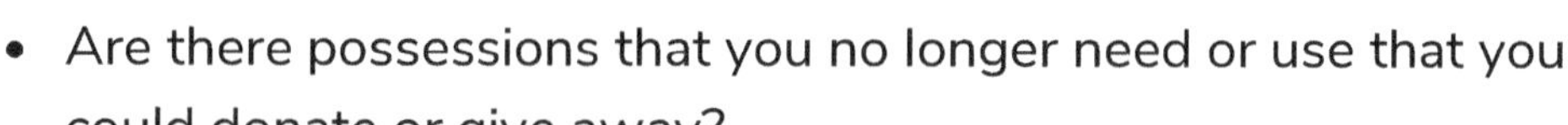

- Are there possessions that you no longer need or use that you could donate or give away?
- Are there relationships that you could invest more time and energy into?

YOUR VALUES

Take a moment to grab a piece of scrap paper and jot down the five most important people or things in your life.

Next, write down the top five activities that occupy the majority of your time.

When you examine your two lists, it's important to ask yourself if the way you're spending your time aligns with your values in your daily life. Our values are the things that we hold most dear. They help us to make sense of the world around us and guide our decisions. Take a reflective pause and consider whether your time is being spent on what truly holds value to your heart.

Sometimes, our schedules can be so overwhelming that we lose sight of what is truly important. One way to ensure that we stay true to our values is to pay attention to how we spend our day. Time is a precious resource, and how we choose to use it reflects our priorities and values. If we spend most of our time on things that don't align with our values, we can begin to feel disconnected from ourselves and our purpose, ultimately impacting our happiness.

Take some time to reflect on your values and how you spend your time. Ask yourself, "What matters most to me? What do I want to prioritize in my life?" Then, evaluate how you currently spend your time. Are there areas where you're not spending enough time on things that matter to you? Are there activities or commitments taking up too much time and not aligning with your values?

YOUR VALUES

Matthew 6:33 says, But seek first his kingdom and his righteousness, and all these things will be given to you as well." This scripture reminds us of the importance of aligning our values with God's kingdom. When we prioritize seeking righteousness and living according to God's principles, everything else falls into place. It reminds us to align our values with God's will through reflection.

Once you've identified areas where you can make changes, plan how to start spending your time in a way that aligns with your values. This might mean saying no to certain commitments or making time for activities that bring you joy and fulfillment.

Living a life that aligns with your values is an ongoing process. You may have to adjust and reevaluate your priorities as you go along. By paying attention to how you spend your time and making intentional choices, you can live a life that is true to your values and brings you purpose.

* What values are most important to you?
* How can you adjust your time to align with the people and things you value the most?

YOUR WHY

Have you ever wondered about your life's purpose? We all have a reason for being here, a unique contribution that only we can make to the world. Yet, sometimes it can feel like we're just going through the motions without a clear sense of direction or purpose.

If you're feeling this way, take heart. You're not alone, and it's never too late to discover your purpose. Your purpose is not always clear, but instead, unfolds as you navigate through life, making choices, and gaining wisdom from your experiences.

To discover your purpose, ask yourself some important questions: What brings you joy and fulfillment? What are your strengths and talents? What are the needs and problems in the world that you're passionate about addressing? By reflecting on these questions, you can begin to get a clearer sense of your purpose and what you're meant to do.

It's important to remember that discovering your purpose is a process, not a destination. You may not find the answers right away, but that's okay. Keep exploring, keep learning, and keep growing. Your purpose will become clearer as you continue on your journey.

God reminds us in Jeremiah 29:11 with the scripture, "For I know the plans I have for you," declares the LORD, "plans to prosper you and not to harm you, plans to give you hope and a future." This verse reminds us that God has a purpose and plan for each of us.

By seeking Him and His guidance, we can discover our true purpose and find fulfillment in living out His plans for our lives. Your purpose will guide you through the ups and downs of life, giving you a sense of direction and meaning. It will help you make important decisions, prioritize your time and energy, and stay true to yourself. Remember, your purpose is unique to you, and only you can fulfill it. You have something valuable to contribute to the world, and the world needs you to show up and share your gifts. So keep searching, keep growing, and never give up on the quest to discover your purpose in life.

- What brings you joy and purpose in life?
- How can you use your strengths and talents to make a positive impact on the world?

SOWING SEEDS

As we go through life, we can sow seeds wherever we go. These seeds can be physical, like planting a garden or giving to charity. They can also be more intangible, like sharing kind words or a smile with someone who's having a tough day. The thing about sowing seeds is that they don't always show results right away. It takes time for them to germinate, grow, and bear fruit. This can be frustrating, especially when we're used to instant gratification. But it's important to remember that every seed we sow has the potential to make a difference, even if we can't see it right away.

In the Bible, Jesus tells a parable about a farmer who went out to sow seeds. A few of the seeds landed on rocky ground and failed to root, while others landed on fertile soil and flourished, yielding a plentiful harvest. You never know which seeds will take root and bear fruit, but that's not for us to decide. Our job is simply to sow as many seeds as we can and trust that some of them will take hold and grow into something beautiful.

2 Corinthians 9:6 says, "Remember this: Whoever sows sparingly will also reap sparingly, and whoever sows generously will also reap generously." Each day presents us with countless chances to sow seeds of kindness and positivity into the lives of those around us. The beauty of these opportunities is that they can be found in the simplest interactions - from the grocery store checkout line to our very own neighborhoods. Consider the moments you've smiled at a stranger, offered a helping hand, or simply listened attentively to a friend in need. These seemingly small gestures can have a profound impact on someone's day, uplifting their spirit and leaving a lasting impression.

SOWING SEEDS

The next time you're feeling discouraged, remember that every seed you sow has the potential to make a difference. Keep sowing, keep planting, and trust that, in time, your efforts will bear fruit. And even if you don't see the results of your labors in this lifetime, know that you're making a difference in the lives of those around you, one seed at a time.

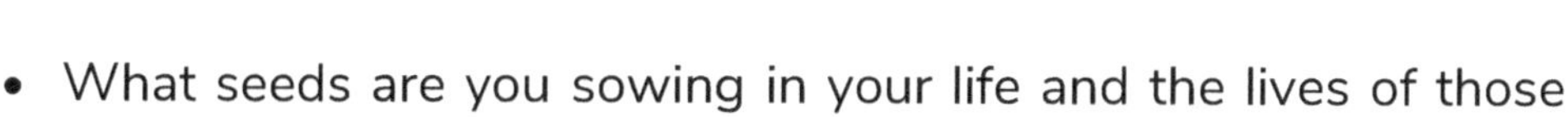

- What seeds are you sowing in your life and the lives of those around you?
- Consider your daily interactions with others. How can you intentionally sow seeds of kindness and positivity in those encounters?

THE POWER OF AFFIRMATIONS

Has anyone said something positive to you or offered you a compliment today? It's remarkable how even the smallest gesture can make a tremendous difference in someone's life. Whether you're standing in line at the grocery store, interacting with your family, or engaging with coworkers, be intentional about seeking opportunities to uplift others. Let your words become a source of inspiration and positivity, spreading joy wherever you go.

Psalm 18:21 tells us that words have the power of life and death. Our words can either build up or tear down, encourage or discourage, affirm or criticize. In our daily lives, it's easy to become entangled in the web of negativity, focusing on what others didn't do or how they fell short of our expectations. We may find ourselves dwelling on why our spouse didn't meet a particular need or why a coworker didn't handle a task the way we envisioned it. However, dwelling in this cycle of negativity only hinders our relationships and robs us of the joy we could experience.

As followers of Christ, we are called to use our words to bring life and to affirm and encourage others. When we affirm others, we not only build them up but also strengthen our relationships with them. Affirming others means acknowledging their strengths, talents, and contributions. It means recognizing the good things they are doing and encouraging them to continue. Affirmation is not flattery or insincere praise, but genuine recognition and appreciation for who they are and what they do.

THE POWER OF AFFIRMATIONS

Looking for the good in people does not mean ignoring their shortcomings. It simply means choosing to build meaningful relationships by showing understanding and providing encouragement. As we intentionally focus on the good in others, we sow seeds of kindness that can transform our interactions and bring joy to our lives. Instead of fixating on what's lacking, let us intentionally seek out the positives in people and acknowledge them.

Jesus Himself modeled affirmation when He said to His disciples in John 15:15, "I no longer call you servants because a servant does not know his master's business. Instead, I have called you friends, for everything that I learned from my Father I have made known to you," He affirmed His disciples as friends and partners in His mission. Positive affirmations create an environment of trust, respect, and appreciation, making individuals feel valued.

As you go about your daily life, consciously affirm those around you and look for the good in others. As you do, you will bring life to those we affirm and experience the joy and blessings that come from building others up.

- Who in your life can you affirm and encourage today?
- How can you consciously use your words to uplift and inspire others?

POCKETS OF GRATITUDE

There is power in appreciating the blessings that fill our lives each day. In a world that often encourages us to focus on what we don't have or what we want, practicing gratitude helps us change our outlook and appreciate what we have in the present moment.

I encourage you to go to YouTube and watch <u>Find Your Gratitude</u> by Sheryl Sandberg. Sheryl discovered the transformative power of gratitude during the process of grieving her husband's passing. Life has a way of reminding us that we are more vulnerable than we ever thought, but it is also in those vulnerable moments that we realize our inherent strength, just like Sheryl did.

Gratitude becomes a guiding light, shining through the darkness and illuminating the path before us. When we intentionally choose gratitude, we invite strength and resilience into our lives, even in the face of adversity. Sheryl encourages us to cultivate a sense of gratitude not just when things are going well, but also during difficult times. It's important to recognize that gratitude can be experienced in any situation, not just under certain circumstances. Expressing gratitude can be a powerful way to change our perspective, redirect our attention, and discover moments of happiness and comfort, even when we face difficult circumstances.

1 Thessalonians 5:18 says, "Give thanks in all circumstances; for this is God's will for you in Christ Jesus." Think about the moments that bring you joy, the relationships that uplift you, and the simple pleasures that brighten your life.

POCKETS OF GRATITUDE

Consider the impact these blessings have on your overall well-being. Gratitude shifts our perspective from scarcity to abundance, from dissatisfaction to contentment. I encourage you to start a gratitude journal and take a moment each night to write down three things you are grateful for during that day. It is a powerful practice that leads to a more fulfilling and joyful life.

- Take a moment to quiet your mind and center your thoughts on gratitude. Reflect on the blessings that you may have taken for granted or overlooked.
- What are three things you are grateful for today, and how can you express that gratitude to others?

LET IT GO

In a world filled with uncertainties and challenges, it's easy to become overwhelmed and consumed by anxious thoughts. However, as followers of Christ, we are called to trust in His provision and find solace in His peace. Through reflection, scripture, and prayer, we can learn to let go of worry and anxiety and discover the freedom and tranquility of surrendering to God's loving embrace.

Worry and anxiety can rob us of peace and hinder our ability to experience God's presence fully. They distract us from living in the present moment and disrupt our connection with Him. Yet, as followers of Christ, we are called to cast our anxieties upon Him, trusting in His faithfulness and care. Letting go of worry and anxiety is not an easy task, but it is a necessary one for our spiritual well-being. It requires surrendering our fears and concerns to God through prayer, petition, and thanksgiving. As we release our burdens, we make room for God's peace to enter our hearts and guard our minds in Christ Jesus.

Philippians 4:6-7 says, "Do not be anxious about anything, but in every situation, by prayer and petition, with thanksgiving, present your requests to God. And the peace of God, which transcends all understanding, will guard your hearts and your minds in Christ Jesus." God invites us to bring our worries before Him, to trust in His provision, and to rest in His unfailing love.

LET IT GO

By shifting your focus from the uncertainties of life to the certainty of His faithfulness, you will find freedom from worry and anxiety. In this surrender, you will discover the peace that surpasses all understanding. Letting go of worry and anxiety is a continuous journey that requires intentional surrender and trust in God's faithfulness. Trust that He holds your concerns in His loving hands and works all things for your good.

- Take a moment to reflect on the worries and anxieties that weigh heavy on your heart. Consider how they affect your thoughts, emotions, and overall well-being.
- How can you release the weight of your worries and surrender them to the guiding hand of God?

SELF CARE

Amidst the chaos of our daily routines, it's easy to neglect our physical and emotional well-being. However, our bodies are precious gifts from God. Taking care of our health is not selfish; it is a responsible act of care and recognition of God's divine plan for our well-being. When we prioritize our health, we are better able to fulfill the purposes that God has for us.

Nurturing our physical bodies through exercise, nourishing foods, and rest gives us the energy and vitality needed to serve others and live out our calling. We can also engage in self-reflection that can foster inner peace, resilience, and a healthy state of mind.

Putting our health first goes beyond physical and mental aspects. It involves nurturing our spiritual well-being as well. Setting aside time for prayer, meditation, and studying scripture allows us to connect with God, derive strength from His presence, and conform our lives to His will. Moments of communion provide the spiritual nourishment and guidance necessary to lead a life that honors God.

If your daily routine involves raising children, taking care of extended family, or managing a demanding job, it can be challenging to find time to focus on your health. However, It's important to make time for yourself. Consider waking up an hour earlier than usual to exercise or meditate. Taking a walk during your lunch break could be a refreshing activity. Find pockets of time in your daily routine to prioritize your physical, mental, and spiritual well-being.

SELF CARE

1 Corinthians 6:19-20 says, "Do you not know that your bodies are temples of the Holy Spirit, who is in you, whom you have received from God? You are not your own; you were bought at a price. Therefore, honor God with your bodies." Putting your health first is an act of stewardship, a way of honoring the gift of life and body entrusted to you by God. As you commit to prioritizing your physical, mental, and spiritual well-being, may you experience the blessings of wholeness in every aspect of your life.

- Take a few moments to reflect on areas of your health that may need attention. Write down practical steps you can take to prioritize your physical, mental, and spiritual well-being.

BUILD MEANINGFUL RELATIONSHIPS

Scripture tells us that we are created for relationships with God and one another. Building meaningful relationships is important for our emotional well-being and our spiritual growth. Meaningful relationships provide support, encouragement, and opportunities for us to learn, grow, and serve together.

Building lasting relationships and connections starts with intentionality. It requires making time for others, actively listening, and being present in their lives. It involves showing empathy, kindness, and compassion, and being willing to share our joys and struggles. John 13:34 states to "Love one another. As I have loved you, so you must love one another." Jesus modeled the importance of building meaningful relationships during His time on Earth. He invested in the lives of His disciples, spending time with them, teaching them, and loving them. He demonstrated genuine care and concern for others, meeting them where they were and offering them hope and grace. To build meaningful relationships, we need to cultivate qualities such as love, forgiveness, humility, and patience. We must be willing to put the needs of others before our own and be open to vulnerability. Meaningful relationships require effort and commitment, but the rewards are immeasurable.

When we build relationships, we create spaces where trust can flourish. We can share our joys and sorrows, our victories and defeats, knowing that we are accepted and loved for who we are. We can walk alongside one another, offering support and encouragement through life's ups and downs.

BUILD MEANINGFUL RELATIONSHIPS

- Are you investing time and energy into building meaningful connections with others?
- Who is one person in your life with whom you desire a more meaningful relationship? How can you take a step towards deepening that connection?

EMBRACE IMPERFECTION

Have you ever found yourself striving for perfection, only to feel overwhelmed and discouraged by your own shortcomings? At times in my life, I have experienced the weight of my imperfections as a student, daughter, spouse, and mother. Throughout my life, I have faced difficulties with body image and the pursuit of an ideal weight and physical appearance as a woman. I'm sure you have experienced the nagging feeling of not quite measuring up to the expectations set by others or even ourselves. The constant comparison can be disheartening and draining.

However, God's grace is more than sufficient to cover our imperfections and insecurities. In fact, it is through our weaknesses that His power is made perfect. It is in those moments when we feel inadequate that God's strength shines brightest. In a world that often values outward perfection, it's important to remember that God's perspective is different. He sees us through the lens of His unconditional love and grace. Our imperfections and weaknesses are not barriers to His presence; rather, they become opportunities for His power to be made perfect in us.

Embracing imperfection is not about settling for mediocrity or neglecting personal growth. Instead, it's a humble recognition that we are finite beings needing God's grace and strength. By recognizing and accepting our limitations, and surrendering them to God, we allow His transformative power to work in our lives.

EMBRACE IMPERFECTION

We may be bombarded with images of flawless beauty, success stories of those who seem to have it all together, and societal pressures to meet unrealistic standards. In a society that often demands perfection, embracing imperfection can be a challenging but liberating choice. 2 Corinthians 12:9 reminds us, "My grace is sufficient for you, for my power is made perfect in weakness." This is a great reminder that His grace is sufficient for us, even in our weaknesses and imperfections.

When we embrace imperfection, we acknowledge our humanity and recognize that we are not meant to be flawless beings. It is through our vulnerabilities that God's power can shine and work in and through us. Release the burden of perfection and embrace the grace that God freely offers. Allow His power to work in and through your weaknesses, knowing that He is with you every step of the way. Trust in His sufficiency and find joy in the journey of embracing imperfection, knowing that you are deeply loved and valued by Him.

- Take a moment to reflect on the times when you've felt imperfect. How have these feelings affected your sense of self-worth?
- Consider how embracing your imperfections can open the door for God's grace and power to work in your life.

Life is full of unexpected twists and turns that catch us off guard. Sometimes these surprises bring us great joy, filling our hearts with excitement and wonder. I can vividly recall a few of these moments in my own life. One such memory takes me back to my 40th birthday party. I had no idea that my husband had planned a surprise celebration for me. As the door opened, a room filled with family and friends erupted in cheers, and my heart swelled with joy. It was a moment I will never forget, a reminder of the joy that can come from the unexpected. Another unforgettable surprise was the day I learned I would be a mother for the first time. The news filled me with a mix of emotions—excitement, fear, and overwhelming joy. At that moment, I realized how life has a way of presenting us with surprises that can transform our lives and bring us immense joy.

Embracing life's surprises is not always easy. I tend to crave control and predictability, seeking comfort in routines and plans. However, when we loosen our grip on expectations and embrace the surprises that come our way, we open ourselves up to a world of joy and wonder. These surprises can be small or life-changing, but they all have the potential to bring us closer to the abundant life God has in store for us.

Jeremiah 29:11 states, "For I know the plans I have for you," declares the Lord, "plans to prosper you and not to harm you, plans to give you hope and a future." Just as God knows His plans for us, we can trust that He orchestrates beautiful surprises along the way.

OPEN YOUR HEART TO SURPRISES

The key is to cultivate an open heart and a spirit of anticipation. Instead of fearing the unknown, choose to find joy in the unexpected, knowing that God's surprises often hold blessings beyond our wildest imaginations.

- Think back to a time when you experienced an unexpected surprise. How did it make you feel, and what did you learn from that experience?
- How can you cultivate a spirit of openness and anticipation for the unexpected surprises that lie ahead?

CARVE YOUR PATH OF PURPOSE

Comparison has a sneaky way of creeping into our lives, robbing us of joy and contentment. There have been countless times when I fell into the trap of comparing myself to others, particularly during my high school years. I often compared my grades with my peers, and it felt like my value as a person was tied to my academic performance. The pressure to excel and meet certain expectations often left me feeling inadequate and robbed me of the joy of learning.

Even in my teaching career, I found myself comparing my teaching methods, achievements, and even the success of my students to other educators. It was a constant battle to resist the urge to compare and embrace my unique journey as a teacher. It took a shift in perspective and a realization that each teacher has their own distinct gifts and talents.

Embracing your unique journey requires letting go of the comparison game. Ephesians 2:10 states, "For we are God's handiwork, created in Christ Jesus to do good works, which God prepared in advance for us to do." We are each wonderfully made with our own set of talents and passions. God has created us with a purpose designed specifically for us to fulfill. When we compare ourselves to others, we diminish the beautiful work that God is doing in and through us.

CARVE YOUR PATH OF PURPOSE

Remember, you are on a journey that is completely your own. Shift your focus from comparing yourself to others and instead acknowledge and celebrate your personal journey. Focus on the progress, growth, and impact you have made in your own unique ways. By embracing your individuality, you can find joy and fulfillment, free from the chains of comparison.

God has a plan and purpose for your life, and it is unlike anyone else's. Embrace your strengths, celebrate your victories, and learn from your challenges. Comparison only hinders your progress, but embracing your unique journey will allow you to flourish and make a meaningful impact in the lives of others.

- Reflect on a time when you caught yourself comparing your life to someone else's. How did it make you feel, and how did it impact your overall sense of joy and contentment?
- What steps can you take to let go of comparison and embrace your unique journey?

CHERISH THE SMALL THINGS

In the complexity of life, it's easy to overlook the simple joys that surround us each day. We often seek happiness in grand accomplishments, big moments, or material possessions, but true joy can be found in the small and seemingly insignificant things that make up our daily lives.

God's creation is filled with beauty and wonder, both in the grandeur of mountains and oceans and in the delicate details of a flower petal or a bird's song. When we pause and take notice of these small blessings, we open ourselves to experiencing joy in its purest form. Jesus often drew attention to the beauty of nature and the ordinary things of life. He spoke of the lilies of the field and the birds of the air, reminding us that God's provision and care extend even to the smallest and seemingly insignificant aspects of creation. In doing so, He invited us to find joy and contentment in the present moment.

Discovering happiness in the little things requires a change in how we perceive the world. This involves taking a moment to pause, being completely in the moment, and fostering a mindset of appreciation. It's about taking notice of the smile on a loved one's face, the warmth of the sun on our skin, or the taste of a delicious meal. It's about finding delight in the simple pleasures that often go unnoticed. When we intentionally seek joy in the small things, we not only enhance our well-being but also inspire others to do the same. Our appreciation for the small blessings can spread like ripples, creating a culture of gratitude and contentment in our homes, workplaces, and communities.

CHERISH THE SMALL THINGS

1 Thessalonians 5:16-18 says, "Rejoice always, pray continually, give thanks in all circumstances; for this is God's will for you in Christ Jesus." This verse reminds us of the importance of rejoicing and giving thanks in all circumstances. It encourages us to find joy in both significant events and ordinary moments of our lives. Be grateful and joyful for the small blessings God gives you each day.

As you go about your day, take a moment to pause and observe the small things that bring you joy. Give thanks for them and allow yourself to be fully present in the moment. Embrace the beauty and wonder surrounding you, and let the simplicity of these small joys fill your heart with gratitude and contentment.

- What is one small thing that brings you joy?
- How can you intentionally seek out and appreciate more of these small joys in your daily life?

BE KIND

Growing up, my dad had lots of sayings. But there is always one I never quite understood until later in life. He would often say… "You get more flies with honey than you do with vinegar." When I was young, I didn't fully grasp the significance behind these simple words. During my teenage years, I conducted an experiment by placing cups of honey and vinegar to determine which one attracted more flies. I observed how the sweetness of honey drew the flies, while the pungent scent of vinegar repelled them. It was a visual representation of the lesson my dad was trying to teach me —kindness can attract and bring people together, while bitterness pushes them away.

This simple saying holds profound truths about the impact of kindness in our lives. Choosing kindness is not always easy, especially when encountering difficult individuals. However, it is during these moments that the power of kindness shines the brightest. Responding to hostility with a gentle word or showing empathy to someone going through a tough time can transform conflicts into opportunities for growth and healing.

In Ephesians 4:32, we are reminded to be kind and compassionate to one another, just as God forgave us through Christ. Our acts of kindness have the potential to create a ripple effect of love and positivity in the lives of others. In our fast-paced and often stressful lives, small acts of kindness can make a world of difference. Offering a smile to a stranger, holding the door open for someone, or lending a listening ear to a friend in need are simple gestures that can brighten someone's day.

BE KIND

Kindness is contagious and has the power to create a positive domino effect. Extending kindness to others can inspire them to pay it forward, creating a ripple effect of goodness that touches many lives. Colossians 3:12 reminds us to "Clothe yourselves with compassion, kindness, humility, gentleness, and patience." These virtues are the essence of a life lived with empathy and love. By embracing these qualities, we can build meaningful connections with others and foster a sense of community and belonging.

Be intentional about incorporating kindness into our daily lives, not just as a fleeting act but as a way of being. By nurturing a culture of kindness and compassion, we can contribute to a more harmonious world, one small act of kindness at a time.

- Reflect on a situation where you could have responded with kindness instead of frustration or impatience. How might a kind response have changed the outcome of that situation?

DON'T SWEAT THE SMALL STUFF

Life can be challenging and unpredictable at times. Simple things like being stuck in traffic, not finding what you need at the grocery store, or having a disagreement with a friend can easily disrupt our balance. Some days, I've allowed the tiniest, most insignificant things to affect my mood for days. These experiences can potentially ruin our day or week if we let them. However, in the grand scheme of things, how significant are these concerns? Will they truly matter in five, ten, or twenty years?

As we journey through life, we encounter various challenges and obstacles that can lead us to stress and anxiety. Matthew 6:34 tells us, "Therefore do not worry about tomorrow, for tomorrow will worry about itself. Each day has enough trouble of its own." The pressures of our daily lives can easily consume us if we let them. Yet, Jesus urges us to focus on the present moment and trust that God has everything under control. Focusing on things that may have caused us distress can deprive us of the happiness and serenity that God wants us to experience. Take a moment to consider the situations that threaten to ruin your day and ask yourself...

Will they truly matter in five years?

Most of our current troubles will fade away with time, replaced by new experiences and growth. In times of uncertainty, pray and cast your cares upon God. Seek His guidance and place your trust in His unfailing love. Embrace each day as a precious gift and let go of the burdens that hinder your journey.

Find comfort in knowing that God walks with us through every season and that His plans are greater than we can imagine. Live in the present, trusting that everything will work together for good in God's perfect timing.

- Think about a recent situation in which a minor event caused you to feel upset. How might you have handled the situation differently if you had considered the question, "Will this matter in five years?"

FIND JOY IN TIMES OF SORROW

In life, there will be moments of sorrow that leave us feeling lost and broken. Sometimes, it may be the disappointment of a job rejection, a failed relationship, or the painful loss of a loved one. A time of sadness occurred in my life when I went through the pain of a miscarriage. The pain and grief felt overwhelming, and it seemed like joy would never find its way back into my life. However, through this dark season, I learned that God has a unique way of bringing joy out of sorrow.

As I wept and mourned the loss of my baby, I clung to God's promises and sought comfort in His unfailing love. In the midst of my sorrow, He whispered words of solace, assuring me that His plans are perfect, even when they don't align with our own. Though my heart was heavy, I trusted that God's favor would eventually replace my pain with joy.

In those moments of despair, I discovered that God is a master at turning our sorrows into songs of praise. He allowed me to find my joy again, not by erasing the memory of my loss, but by healing my broken heart and restoring my spirit. God's grace, like a gentle sunrise, brought hope and renewal to my soul.

A year later, as I continued to walk with Him through my grief, God blessed me with another pregnancy. My joy was restored as I carried this new life within me, a living testament to God's faithfulness and His promise of renewal. This precious child became a symbol of hope, reminding me that even in the midst of sadness, God is always working for our good.

FIND JOY IN TIMES OF SORROW

Psalm 30:5 states, "For his anger lasts only a moment, but his favor lasts a lifetime; weeping may stay for the night, but rejoicing comes in the morning." God understands our sorrows intimately and is ever-present to carry us through the darkest nights. In our moments of despair, remember that weeping may endure for the night, but joy comes in the morning. Like a skilled potter, God molds beauty out of brokenness, turning our sorrow into songs of thanksgiving.

- In what ways can you trust God's plan and find hope in His promises, even amidst heartache and disappointment?

WELCOME CHANGE AND UNCERTAINTY

Consistency is a defining trait of mine. Change has never been my ally; I thrive on structure. From waking up at a fixed hour to sticking to familiar meals, my days follow a predictable rhythm. I take solace in the familiarity of my daily routine, embracing the sense of stability it provides. As time has passed, I've realized that life is an adventure full of unexpected twists and turns, surprises, and phases of transformation. It is in these moments of transition and uncertainty that we may feel apprehensive, fearful, or hesitant to let go of the familiar and embrace the unknown. However, as followers of Christ, we are called to trust in the Lord and lean on His faithfulness, even during times of uncertainty.

There were moments in my life when I changed professions, moved to a different city, or anticipated the birth of a child, during which I experienced uncertainty about what the future would hold. But as I put my trust in God, I discovered that His provision and guidance opened doors I never expected. As much as I cherished my structured life, I discovered that the unpredictable nature of life often leads to the greatest blessings. Letting go of my expectations allowed me to welcome unexpected opportunities and find joy in the surprises that unfolded.

Embracing change and uncertainty requires us to surrender our plans and place our trust in God's hands. It is through these seasons that our faith is strengthened, and our dependence on Him deepens. As we submit our lives to His leading, we can rest assured that He will direct us toward His purpose and bring about blessings even during seasons of change.

WELCOME CHANGE AND UNCERTAINTY

In times of transition and uncertainty, cling to the truth of Proverbs 3:5-6. "Trust in the LORD with all your heart and lean not on your own understanding; in all your ways submit to him, and he will make your paths straight." Submit to Him in every area of your life, embracing change with faith and confidence, knowing He is faithful to guide, provide, and bring beauty from ashes.

- Recall a specific moment of change or uncertainty in your life. How did God reveal His faithfulness to you during that time?
- What change or uncertainty are you facing right now, and how can you trust God's guidance and provision through it?

SERVE OTHERS

In a world that often promotes self-interest and personal gain, the call to serve others is a testament to the transformative power of selflessness and love. Serving others requires a mindset shift from self-centeredness to an outward focus. It challenges us to set aside our desires, ambitions, and agendas and instead seek opportunities to meet the needs of those around us. Think about the times when you have selflessly served others, whether through acts of kindness, helping, or sacrificing your time. In those moments, you have likely experienced the profound fulfillment that comes from investing in others and making a positive difference in their lives. It is in this selflessness that we find true fulfillment and purpose.

Mark 10:45 reminds us that "For even the Son of Man came not to be served but to serve, and to give his life as a ransom for many." When we serve others, we participate in God's redemptive work. We become instruments of His grace, bringing hope to the brokenhearted, comfort to the weary, and healing to the wounded. It is through acts of service that we embody the love of Christ and become His hands and feet in a hurting world.

Remember that serving others is not solely limited to grand gestures or high-profile endeavors. It can be as simple as a kind word, a listening ear, or a small act of kindness. Every opportunity to serve, no matter how big or small, is significant in God's eyes. By serving others, we align ourselves with the heart of Christ and become vessels of His love in a hurting world.

SERVE OTHERS

Serving others is not always convenient or easy. It may require sacrifice, humility, and stepping out of our comfort zones. However, the blessings that flow from serving far outweigh any temporary inconvenience. You will experience a profound sense of fulfillment, appreciation, and purpose as you dedicate yourself to serving others.

- How can you actively seek opportunities to serve others daily in your family, workplace, or community?

RISE ABOVE FEAR

When we enter this world, fear becomes a constant companion on our journey. Reflect for a moment on the earliest memories of fear in your life. It's likely that you have to go back to your very first days when the safety and warmth of your mother's womb shielded you from any worries or concerns. As soon as we are born into this world, fear swiftly enters our lives. As a child, I feared dark rooms, being alone, and strangers. The fears continued to grow as I faced the challenges of school, the pressure to please others, the sting of rejection, and the discomfort of being different.

In fact, I have encountered moments of fear that have left lasting imprints. One such memory takes me back to the devastating events of September 11th, 2001. That day shattered my sense of safety when our country was attacked. Fear revealed its power, exposing how it can grip our thoughts and shape our reactions during times of crisis.

The truth is, we are all afraid of something. Our fears can influence our actions more than we realize, dictating how we navigate life's challenges. Fear of rejection, failure, disappointment, or inadequacy can hold us back, preventing us from fully embracing our dreams and embracing who we truly are. Many people find themselves trapped in the fear of time. They wait for the "perfect" moment to pursue their dreams, whether it's going back to school, starting a new job, getting married, or starting a family. But time waits for no one, and the fear of missing out can paralyze us if we let it. It's important to reflect on our fears to understand how they shape our lives and limit our potential.

RISE ABOVE FEAR

2 Timothy 1:7 says, "For God has not given us a spirit of fear, but of power and of love and of a sound mind." This scripture reminds us that fear does not come from God. Instead, God provides us with the power, love, and a sound mind to face and overcome our fears. It serves as a reminder that we can find strength and courage in Him to live a life free from the bondage of fear.

By acknowledging your fears and embracing courage, you can break free from their grip and seize the opportunities that await you. While you may never completely eliminate fear, you can choose how to respond. Remember, fear may be present, but it doesn't have to define you. You can choose your actions and live a life guided by love, purpose, and resilience.

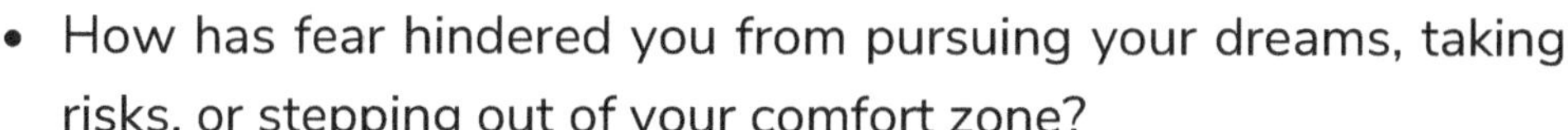

- How has fear hindered you from pursuing your dreams, taking risks, or stepping out of your comfort zone?
- How can you rely on God's love and guidance to overcome fear and step into a life of courage and fulfillment?

EAT ALONE

Have you ever sat alone at a restaurant to eat? For the longest time, I avoided this experience, thinking it was something to pity or even fear. I was curious about how individuals could have a meal by themselves without feeling lonely or uneasy. It wasn't until my late thirties that I discovered the beauty and confidence of embracing solitude.

In a world that often emphasizes companionship and social interactions, the act of eating alone can be perceived as strange. We may assume that those dining solo have few connections or are somehow lacking in their lives. Yet, consider the courage it takes for an individual to sit alone in a restaurant, fully aware of the potential judgments and assumptions of others. They could easily opt for takeout and retreat to the comfort of their own space, shielded from prying eyes. Yet, by choosing to eat alone in public, they assert their confidence and self-worth.

I've come to understand that eating alone doesn't necessarily mean feeling isolated or lonely. It is an act of self-reflection, allowing us to engage in introspection, gather our thoughts, and find solace in our own company. It is a deliberate choice to prioritize our own well-being and inner peace. When we are unafraid to spend time alone, we recognize that our thoughts, feelings, and reflections are valuable companions. We choose to nourish ourselves physically, mentally, and spiritually, using solitude as an opportunity for personal growth and self-discovery.

Psalm 139:13-14 says, "For you formed my inward parts; you knitted me together in my mother's womb. I praise you, for I am fearfully and wonderfully made. Wonderful are your works; my soul knows it very well." Remember that we are fearfully and wonderfully made by a loving Creator who knows the intricate details of our being. Our worth is not determined by the company we keep but by the inherent value bestowed upon us. Whether you're spending time with friends or enjoying a meal alone, it's important to feel comfortable and confident in your own presence. Remember that you are deserving of love, respect, and appreciation.

- How can embracing solitude enhance your self-awareness and personal growth?

CHERISH THE JOURNEY

Do you find yourself placing your happiness solely on the outcomes of life? Perhaps you eagerly await graduation day, the completion of a project, or the fulfillment of a long-awaited dream, believing that true joy will only come once those outcomes are achieved. In doing so, we often overlook the beauty and significance of the process.

I dedicated months to meticulously planning my wedding day, only to spend the entire year leading up to it stressed and overwhelmed. My focus became fixated on that one day while disregarding the joy and growth that can be found within the journey itself. We may love the idea of holding a diploma but dread the hours of studying and hard work required to attain it.

The problem with this mindset is that it robs us of the joy and fulfillment that can be found in every step of the process. By fixating solely on the outcome, we miss the valuable lessons, personal growth, and memorable moments that shape us along the way. We inadvertently place our happiness on hold, convinced that it will only be accessible once we reach the desired destination.

However, the truth is that happiness should not be dependent on outcomes. Our joy should not be tied solely to the end result, but rather rooted in the present moment and the journey itself. When we learn to appreciate the process, we discover a wellspring of contentment and gratitude that sustains us through both the highs and lows.

CHERISH THE JOURNEY

Romans 8:28 says, "And we know that for those who love God, all things work together for good, for those who are called according to his purpose." Remember that God works in mysterious and marvelous ways and is not solely concerned with the final outcome. He is deeply invested in the process, working out the intricate details of our lives to shape us and fulfill His purposes. As we learn to trust Him, we can find joy and peace even amidst uncertainty and setbacks, knowing that He is at work, weaving together a beautiful tapestry.

Find joy in the small victories, the growth, and the lessons learned along the way. Rather than obsessing over reaching our destination, we should enjoy and appreciate the present moment, with the assurance that God's goodness and faithfulness guide us every step of the journey. Today, choose to detach your happiness from outcomes. Embrace the journey with a grateful heart, finding joy as you trust God's guidance and provision.

- Consider a goal or dream you are currently pursuing. How can you find joy in the process and celebrate each step along the way?

CHOOSE JOY

As you navigate through the busyness of daily life, what captures your attention each day? Your focus may be a stay-at-home mom, a caregiver for a loved one, or a devoted employee at your job. Our daily routines can easily consume our thoughts and energy, leaving little room for intentional joy and gratitude.

During my career in education, I found myself in a stressful job, not because of the nature of the work itself, but due to the dysfunctional work environment. The team I worked with lacked trust, effective communication, and genuine camaraderie. It often led to tough conversations and left me feeling drained and upset. Every morning, I would wake up dreading the day ahead and anxiously anticipate the end of the workday. However, I had an epiphany that my negative attitude was only making the situation worse. Instead of solely focusing on the negatives, I needed to intentionally seek out the good things within my job. I realized there were blessings and valuable lessons that I was missing by fixating on the negative aspects of my job.

So, I decided to change my habits and mindset. Each morning I began acknowledging all the positive aspects of my job. I expressed gratitude for the opportunities it provided. Every night, I started the habit of jotting down three things that I appreciated or moments that brought me happiness throughout the day in my gratitude journal. In our daily life, it's important not to fixate solely on the negative aspects of our situation.

CHOOSE JOY

Gradually, as I shifted my thinking, my life and conditions improved. I discovered that when we focus on the good, more good is attracted into our lives. By waking up a few minutes earlier to set our minds in a positive direction, listening to uplifting messages during the day, and reflecting on moments of joy in the evening, we can transform our outlook and cultivate a life filled with gratitude and joy.

1 Thessalonians 5:16-18 reminds us to "Rejoice always, pray continually, give thanks in all circumstances; for this is God's will for you in Christ Jesus." Today, I encourage you to consciously shift your focus toward the positive aspects of your life, no matter how small or seemingly insignificant. Begin your day with a mindset of gratitude and affirmations of the blessings around you. Throughout the day, intentionally seek out uplifting messages and moments of joy. And at night, take a moment to reflect and express gratitude for the joy-filled moments that have brightened your day.

Remember, as you choose joy and shift your focus, you create an atmosphere where more goodness can flourish. Embrace this transformative mindset and experience its profound impact on your life and relationships.

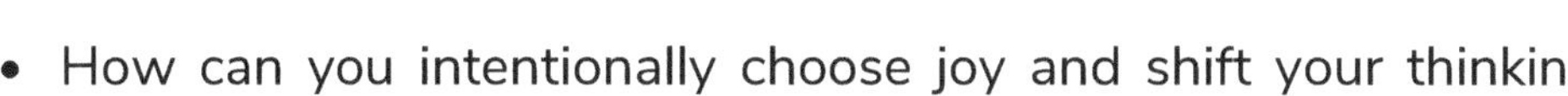

- How can you intentionally choose joy and shift your thinking toward the positive aspects of your daily life?

SEE THE GOOD IN OTHERS

Have you ever stopped to consider how you perceive others? Various factors, including our own experiences, biases, and beliefs, can influence our interactions with people. It's essential to reflect on how we see and approach others; it shapes our relationships and impacts the world around us.

I conducted a research experiment for graduate school after learning about the "law of attraction." This concept suggests that our beliefs and focus can shape our reality. Intrigued by its potential, I decided to put it to the test. My research question was, "Did my attitude and emotions as a teacher impact my students' achievement?" As part of my experiment, I intentionally chose my 4th-period class. Those students were by far my worst-behaved group of students, and I wanted to see if my attitude toward them would change their behavior and academics. For nine weeks, I choose to focus on their positive qualities and to extend grace and compassion in my interactions. Instead of scolding students for not doing their homework or bringing a pencil to class, I changed my language to express belief in their ability to come prepared next time.

The results were astounding.

Not only did I notice a shift in how I perceived my students, but I also witnessed a transformation in my relationships with them. By choosing to see the good in my students, I was able to cultivate deeper connections, foster understanding, and promote a more positive culture.

SEE THE GOOD IN OTHERS

In a world where many people can be mean and rude, it's important for us to make a conscious effort to respond to others in a kind manner. We can choose to see beyond surface-level judgments and embrace a perspective of grace and compassion. When we extend kindness, forgiveness, and understanding, we create an atmosphere encouraging growth, healing, and transformation.

God's Word reminds us to be kind and compassionate, just as He has shown us kindness and forgiveness. Ephesians 4:32 says, "Be kind and compassionate to one another, forgiving each other, just as in Christ God forgave you." By following His example, we can sow seeds of love, acceptance, and empathy in our interactions. As we shift our perspective to see others through grace, we contribute to building a more compassionate and inclusive community.

Reflect on how you see others. Are you quick to judge, criticize, or overlook their worth? Or do you choose to see their inherent value, potential, and unique qualities? As you intentionally shift your focus to see the good in others, you will open yourself to experiencing deeper connections and the transformative power of love.

* Take a moment to reflect on how you feel when someone sees and acknowledges the best in you. How can you cultivate a similar approach in your interactions with others?

CELEBRATE PROGRESS...NOT PERFECTION

In our pursuit of success and growth, we often strive for perfection. We set high standards for ourselves and focus on achieving perfect results in every aspect of our lives. However, this relentless pursuit of perfection can lead to frustration, disappointment, and a constant sense of falling short.

But what if we shifted our perspective and celebrated progress instead of perfection? What if we recognized that the journey itself is filled with small victories and significant growth? In Philippians, the apostle Paul reminds us that he has not yet achieved his ultimate goal nor obtained all that he desires. Yet, he presses on, embracing the process and the progress made along the way.

Over the years, I have learned that perfection is an unattainable standard. Instead, I have learned to appreciate the steps I have taken, the lessons learned, and the growth I have experienced. Celebrating progress allows us to recognize and affirm the efforts we have made, regardless of how small they may seem. It enables us to find joy in the journey and to appreciate the transformation.

Whether it is in your personal relationships, professional endeavors, or spiritual growth, take time to celebrate the milestones you have achieved, the challenges you have overcome, and the positive changes you have made. Every step forward, no matter how small, brings us closer to becoming the person God has called us to be.

CELEBRATE PROGRESS...NOT PERFECTION

Today, let go of the burden of perfection and celebrate your progress. Philippians 1:6 says, "And I am certain that God, who began the good work within you, will continue his work until it is finally finished on the day when Christ Jesus returns." Just as a sculptor molds clay into a masterpiece, God shapes and molds us into the likeness of His Son, Jesus Christ. He has begun a good work within you, and He is faithful to continue it until the day of completion.

- Are you more focused on perfection or progress? Consider the areas where you have grown and changed over time.
- How has God been at work within you? What victories and milestones can you celebrate, no matter how small they may seem?

LET YOUR LIGHT SHINE

There have been moments in my life when I allowed fear, self-doubt, and the opinions of others to dim the light within me. I held back from embracing my unique gifts, talents, and passions, fearing that they were not worthy or important enough. However, God has called each one of us to let our light shine brightly in this world. When we let our light shine, we radiate God's love, grace, and truth to those around us. It is through our actions, words, and attitudes that we have the opportunity to make a positive impact on others and bring glory to our Heavenly Father. We are not called to hide or diminish our light, but to share it confidently with the world.

It is understandable that we may feel hesitant or unsure at times. I even felt that uncertainty as I was writing the very book you are reading right now. I questioned my abilities and thought about how others might perceive it. But I had to remind myself that the light within me is not of my own making; it is a reflection of God's presence and goodness in my life. The same principle applies to you. When we embrace our true identity as children of God, we can shine with confidence and purpose.

Letting our light shine begins with self-acceptance of the unique gifts and talents that God has bestowed upon us. Matthew 5:16 states, "In the same way, let your light shine before others, that they may see your good deeds and glorify your Father in heaven." We are fearfully and wonderfully made with a divine purpose to fulfill. By recognizing and embracing our strengths, passions, and values, we can align our lives with God's calling and make a meaningful difference in the world.

LET YOUR LIGHT SHINE

As we step out in faith and let our light shine, we inspire and encourage others to do the same. Our actions of kindness, compassion, and service can ignite a spark of hope and transformation in the lives of those we encounter. By letting our light shine, we become beacons of God's love, pointing others toward Him.

Today, choose to let your light shine. Embrace your God-given purpose and share your unique gifts with the world. Allow the light within you to illuminate the lives of others, pointing them toward the love and truth of our Heavenly Father. Remember that as you let your light shine, you not only bless others but also bring glory to God.

- What are your unique gifts, talents, and passions? In what ways have you allowed fear or self-doubt to dim your light?
- How can you use your gifts and passions to make a positive impact in your family, community, or workplace?

THE POWER OF LAUGHTER

Laughter has an incredible power to uplift our spirits, brighten our days, and strengthen our connections with others. It is a gift that brings joy and healing to our hearts. I have experienced some of my most precious moments of laughter in the company of my family, engaging in silly activities and creating lasting memories.

When we engage in lighthearted moments and allow ourselves to let go of inhibitions, we open ourselves up to the sheer delight of laughter. It is in those moments of pure joy that we experience a deep connection with our loved ones and create bonds that last a lifetime. Whether it's taking part in a silly challenge, sharing funny GIFs in a group chat, or reminiscing on childhood memories, these moments of laughter bring us closer together and strengthen the ties that bind us.

Laughter has a profound impact on our well-being. Provers 17:22 states, "A joyful heart is good medicine, but a crushed spirit dries up the bones." Laughter is the best medicine because it has the power to reduce stress, release tension, and boost our mood. It is a natural remedy that lightens our burdens and gives our souls a sense of relief. Laughter creates an atmosphere of warmth and positivity. It brings light into the darkest corners and turns ordinary moments into extraordinary ones. In difficult times, laughter provides a much-needed break, a moment of genuine joy that revitalizes and reinvigorates us.

THE POWER OF LAUGHTER

When we share laughter with our family, friends, and even strangers, we spread the contagious joy that ripples through our relationships and touches the lives of others. It becomes a powerful force that transforms the ordinary into the extraordinary. Seek out moments of silliness and playfulness with your loved ones. Create traditions that spark laughter and bring you closer together. Share funny stories, jokes, or experiences that light up the room with laughter. In doing so, we nourish our souls and create a legacy of joy for generations to come.

- What are some of your most cherished moments of laughter and joy?
- How has laughter brought you closer to your friends or family
- How can you intentionally incorporate more laughter into your relationships and daily life?

PROTECT YOUR PEACE

Throughout our lives, there will be moments when we allow the opinions of others or challenging circumstances to steal our inner peace. The fear of judgment and worrying about what others might think can be a source of stress. When we constantly seek validation from others and base our worth on their opinions, we become vulnerable to losing our peace. We cannot control what others think of us, nor should we derive our value solely from their approval. Our worth is rooted in God's unconditional love and acceptance of us as His beloved children.

Being intentional about the inputs we allow into our lives is crucial in safeguarding our peace. The media we consume, the relationships we nurture, and the environments we expose ourselves to can greatly impact our inner serenity. Choosing to surround ourselves with positivity, uplifting influences, and God's truth helps to protect our peace and guard against the negative influences that seek to steal it away.

Protecting your peace begins by cultivating a steadfast and unwavering trust in God. When our minds are anchored in Him, and our confidence is rooted in His faithfulness, we can experience a deep sense of peace that remains unshaken by the storms of life. Isaiah 26:3 says, "You will keep in perfect peace those whose minds are steadfast because they trust in you." When we trust in God's providence and surrender our worries to Him, we can experience peace even in the midst of chaos.

PROTECT YOUR PEACE

One way to safeguard our peace is to release the burden of others' opinions. Instead of allowing external judgments to consume our thoughts and emotions, we can turn to God in prayer and surrender our concerns to Him. By entrusting our worries and insecurities to Him, we open ourselves to His peace that surpasses all understanding.

In prayer, you can seek God's guidance and ask Him to grant you the wisdom and discernment to focus on His truth rather than the opinions of others. You can ask for strength to overcome the fear of judgment and know that your Creator fearfully and wonderfully made you.

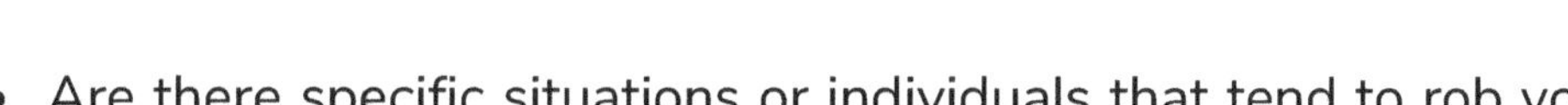

- Are there specific situations or individuals that tend to rob you of your tranquility?
- What steps can you take to embrace the peace that comes from living according to God's truth?

THE POWER OF FORGIVENESS

Throughout our lives, there will be moments when we experience hurt and betrayal at the hands of others. In those moments, it's natural to feel anger, resentment, and bitterness towards those who we believe have wronged us. However, holding onto these negative emotions can weigh us down and hinder our journey toward peace and freedom.

I can recall times in my own life when I clung to bitterness, allowing it to poison my heart and thoughts. The grudges I held against others consumed my energy and hindered my ability to experience joy and inner peace. It was as if I was carrying a heavy burden that only weighed me down, keeping me from moving forward.

But the truth is, harboring resentment only perpetuates the cycle of pain and keeps us captive to the past. It robs us of the freedom and abundant life God desires for us. In contrast, forgiveness can release us from the shackles of bitterness and open our hearts to healing and restoration.

Forgiveness is not an easy process; it does not mean condoning or forgetting the hurt caused. Instead, it involves a conscious decision to release the grip of bitterness and entrust healing and justice to God. Colossians 3:13 call us to "Bear with each other and forgive one another if any of you has a grievance against someone. Forgive as the Lord forgave you." Just as the Lord has forgiven us of our sins, we are called to extend forgiveness to others.

THE POWER OF FORGIVENESS

Today, make a conscious choice to embrace the power of forgiveness. Release the burden of bitterness and resentment, and invite God's healing and restoration into your heart. Remember that forgiveness is a process, and it may require ongoing surrender and prayer. As you extend grace and forgiveness, you will experience the freedom and peace that comes from embracing God's love and His plan for your life.

- Are there individuals or situations from your past that still evoke negative emotions? Have you considered how keeping these emotions has impacted your overall well-being and your relationships?
- How might extending forgiveness bring about healing, freedom, and restoration in your heart and relationships?

LOOK FOR THE SWEET THINGS

Are you a bird watcher? Have you ever taken a moment to observe the birds and their fascinating behaviors? Consider the contrast between vultures and hummingbirds. Vultures are known for their keen insight and ability to spot dead things from miles away. They hover over fields and roads, preying on the lifeless. On the other hand, hummingbirds gather and fly over sweet things. They seek out landscapes adorned with vibrant flowers, finding delight in the sweetness of life.

In their journeys over diverse landscapes, both vultures and hummingbirds may encounter flowers and dead animals. However, they each have a distinct focus and purpose. As humans, we can learn valuable lessons from these animals. Some individuals embody the characteristics of vultures, constantly gravitating toward the negative and focusing on the gloomy aspects of life. On the other hand, there are those who bear a resemblance to hummingbirds, exuding happiness and embracing the brighter aspects of life.

Your perspective and mindset play a crucial role in shaping your experiences. If you have a negative mindset and only expect feelings of despair and sadness, chances are high that you will encounter those emotions. Conversely, if you choose to adopt a positive outlook and believe that good things will unfold in your day, you will discover them. The way you look at life determines your experience of it.

LOOK FOR THE SWEET THINGS

Philippians 4:8 says, "Finally, brothers and sisters, whatever is true, whatever is noble, whatever is right, whatever is pure, whatever is lovely, whatever is admirable—if anything is excellent or praiseworthy—think about such things." God calls us to fix our thoughts on true, noble, right, pure, lovely, admirable, excellent, and praiseworthy things. When you focus your thoughts on positive things, you allow happiness, thankfulness, and an increased understanding of the good things in your life to come in.

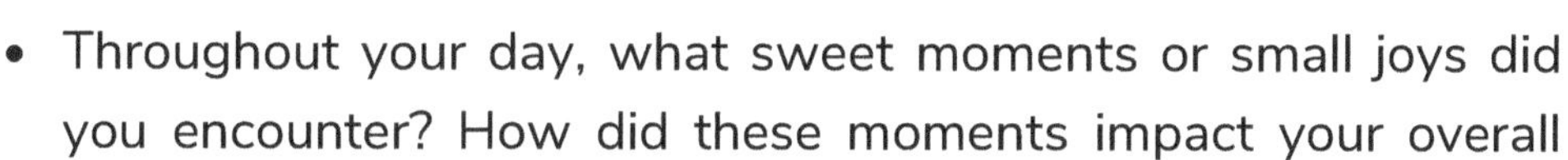

- Throughout your day, what sweet moments or small joys did you encounter? How did these moments impact your overall mood and perspective?
- In challenging situations, how can you intentionally look for the "sweet things" or positive aspects? How might embracing gratitude for these sweet moments influence your response to difficult circumstances?

ENJOY THE OUTDOORS

Amidst the busyness of life, there is a serene place that my husband and I retreat to every evening—the great outdoors. As the day winds down, we find solace in sitting outside and savoring precious moments together. For us, it's a sacred space where we connect on a deeper level, nurturing our relationship amidst the beauty of nature.

From our favorite spot, we watch our children play and often chat with neighbors. These moments in nature remind us of the importance of being present and fully embracing the beauty surrounding us. Psalm 46:10 says, "Be still, and know that I am God." These precious moments outsides offer an opportunity to slow down, to be still, and to recognize the divine presence in our lives. As we immerse ourselves in the sights and sounds of the natural world, we find restoration, peace, and a sense of connection to something greater than ourselves.

Getting outside and exposing yourself to natural sunlight is also a great way to boost your vitamin D levels. The production of vitamin D in your skin is initiated by sunlight, which is crucial for your physical and emotional well-being. As you create an intentional space to sit outside and soak in the wonders of nature, allow yourself to be fully present in the moment. Breathe in the air, listen to the gentle whispers of the wind, and embrace the beauty unfolding before you. Let these tranquil moments become a source of renewal, reminding you of the simple joys and the precious gift of each day.

ENJOY THE OUTDOORS

Consider the times you have savored outdoor moments with loved ones or relished the beauty of sunsets.

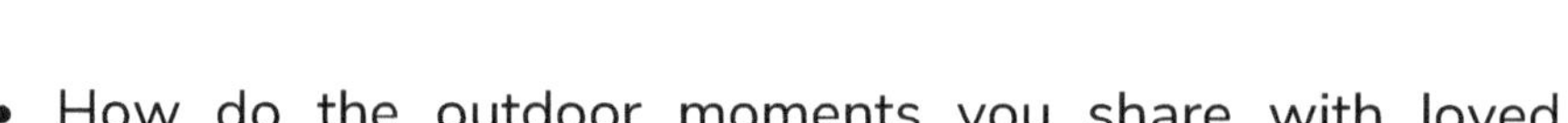

- How do the outdoor moments you share with loved ones enhance your sense of connection and deepen your relationships?
- What other practices or activities can you incorporate into your daily routine to fully embrace the peacefulness and beauty of nature?

EVERY SEASON SERVES A PURPOSE

There are seasons in life that test our strength, challenge our faith, and push us beyond our limits. One such season for me was when I found myself on bed rest during my pregnancy. It was a time of immense physical limitations and emotional uncertainty. Yet, looking back, I can see how God was at work, shaping and molding me in the midst of it all.

Being confined to a bed for an extended period may seem like a wasted season, filled with frustration and restlessness. However, it was during those moments of stillness that I learned the power of surrender and trust. I had to release my own plans and expectations, leaning on God's strength and provision.

In the quiet solitude of those days, I found solace in His presence. I discovered the beauty of prayer, reflection, and listening to His gentle whispers. It was in that season of physical stillness that my spirit grew stronger, and my faith deepened. God was shaping me, molding my character, and preparing me for the journey ahead.

In life, we often find ourselves longing for the next season, wishing to fast-forward to what lies ahead. We compare our current stage to the achievements of others, feeling discontented with where we are.

But what if we learned to appreciate and embrace every season of our journey?

EVERY SEASON SERVES A PURPOSE

Ecclesiastes 3:1 says, "There is a time for everything, and a season for every activity under the heavens." Consider the changing seasons in nature. Each one serves a purpose and holds its own beauty. Spring brings new beginnings, growth, and hope. Summer is a season of abundance and vibrancy. Autumn offers the beauty of transformation and letting go. Winter invites us to slow down, reflect, and find inner warmth.

As you come to recognize the value and significance of each stage in your life's journey, you will develop a sense of gratitude, satisfaction, and a better comprehension of God's unwavering devotion. Embrace where you are, trust in His perfect timing, and find joy in each step along the way.

- In what season of life do you find yourself right now? How can you appreciate and embrace the specific joys and challenges it brings?
- Consider the seasons you have already journeyed through. Reflect on the lessons and growth you experienced during each one. How have they shaped you into who you are today?

At one point in my life, I found myself caught up in the demands of working two jobs as a teacher, constantly striving to make ends meet, and feeling like I was trapped in a never-ending rat race. The days blurred together as I rushed from one task to another, often neglecting my own well-being and the things that truly mattered.

In the midst of the busyness and exhaustion, I realized that I was merely existing, losing sight of the purpose and joy that should accompany my work. I longed for a life that went beyond the paycheck-to-paycheck routine and allowed me to experience a deeper sense of fulfillment.

It was during this time that God reminded me to seek His kingdom and righteousness first. He showed me that true freedom and purpose are found when we align our priorities with His plans. Rather than running endlessly after worldly success and financial security, I needed to trust His provision and seek His guidance for my life.

John 10:10 says, "The thief comes only to steal and kill and destroy; I have come that they may have life and have it to the full." Through prayer and reflection, I realize God created us for a purpose, and He desires us to live a life of fullness, joy, and fulfillment. It's not enough to exist; we are called to truly live, to embrace each day as a gift, and to pursue our passions and dreams with courage and faith.

I realized that my worth was not defined by the number of hours I worked or the amount of money I earned, but by the impact I had on others and the alignment of my life with God's purposes. I let go of the unnecessary busyness and embraced a more balanced approach to work and life. I have found that when I give up my worries and fears to God, I am able to experience a feeling of peace and contentment even when I am faced with difficult situations.

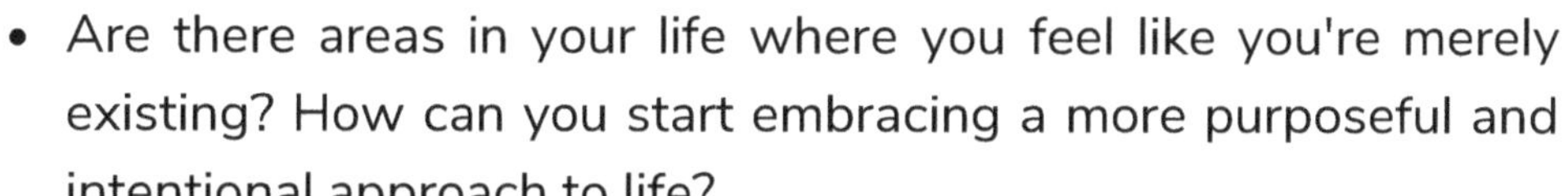

- Are there areas in your life where you feel like you're merely existing? How can you start embracing a more purposeful and intentional approach to life?
- Reflect on the moments when you felt most alive and fulfilled. What were you doing? What passions or dreams were you pursuing? How can you incorporate more of those elements into your daily life?

CHASE YOUR DREAMS

In life, we all have dreams and aspirations that ignite a fire within us. They beckon us to pursue them with unwavering determination and unyielding passion. One of the most inspiring examples of chasing dreams comes from my own son's journey.

When my son didn't make his middle school basketball team, he could have let disappointment extinguish his dreams. Instead, he chose to channel that setback into fuel for his ambition. Every day, he dedicated himself to honing his skills, practicing tirelessly, and pushing past his limits. He was relentless in his pursuit of improvement, knowing that his dream of becoming a better basketball player was within his grasp.

Through his unwavering commitment, my son demonstrated the power of persistence. He embraced the challenges, setbacks, and hard work required to chase his dream. He understood at an early age, that true success is not found in immediate results but in the journey itself.

Proverbs 16:3 says, "Commit to the Lord whatever you do, and he will establish your plans." Let this verse remind you that as you chase your dreams, commit them to God. Trust in His guidance and surrender your plans to Him. With God's help, you can overcome obstacles, find strength in setbacks, and experience the fulfillment that comes from pursuing your dreams wholeheartedly.

CHASE YOUR DREAMS

You may have dreams of launching your own business, writing a book, or traveling the world. Whatever your dreams may be, let them ignite a fire within you, propelling you forward with unwavering determination. Embrace the journey, overcome obstacles, and never cease to chase the dreams that whisper to your soul.

Remember, chasing your dreams is not merely about achieving a specific outcome. It's about embracing the journey, growing through challenges, and becoming the person you were created to be. So, set your sights on the dreams that set your soul on fire and chase them with unwavering faith, perseverance, and joy.

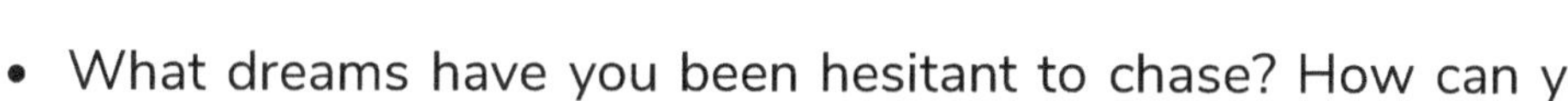

- What dreams have you been hesitant to chase? How can you commit to pursuing them with greater determination?
- What setbacks or challenges have you faced on your journey? How can you use them as stepping stones toward your dreams?

BE PATIENT

In our fast-paced world, patience often feels like a scarce virtue. We yearn for instant results and quick fixes, fearing that time might slip away from us. However, the most beautiful things in life often require patience. Just like the process of a butterfly's transformation, there are moments when we must allow things to unfold naturally.

When I was pregnant with my daughter, I was filled with anticipation and wonder as I eagerly awaited her arrival. During those nine months, I felt very impatient, longing to hold my baby girl. However, it is in this waiting period that we learn valuable lessons about trust and the beauty of anticipation.

Romans 8:25 says, "But if we hope for what we do not yet have, we wait for it patiently." Patience teaches us to trust in divine timing and surrender control to a higher power. It allows for growth, refinement, and the unfolding of God's plan in our lives. Rather than rushing to grasp the outcome, embrace the journey and find joy in the present moment.

Consider the times when you had to exercise patience in your own life. Perhaps it was pursuing a long-term goal or waiting for a desired outcome. It could have been nurturing a relationship, healing from a challenging situation, or embarking on a personal transformation. In each of these instances, patience played a crucial role.

BE PATIENT

Patience nurtures resilience, strengthens our character, and teaches us to trust in divine timing. Reflect on the lessons you learned during those periods of waiting. Recall the emotions, the doubts, and the moments of resilience. Recognize the progress you've made as you learn to be patient and accept the natural progression of things.

- Can you recall a specific instance in your life when impatience led to undesirable outcomes? What lessons did you learn from that experience?
- How can you cultivate patience in your daily life and trust in the perfect timing of things?

TIME HEALS

Time has a remarkable way of healing wounds, soothing sorrows, and restoring our lives. It carries within it the gift of gradual transformation, allowing us to heal, grow, and find solace in the midst of life's challenges.

There are moments in our lives when we may feel overwhelmed by pain, loss, or heartache. It can be difficult to imagine a future where the wounds will no longer sting and the scars will fade. Yet, time holds within it the promise of healing and renewal. I have personally experienced the healing power of time in my own journey. At times, the pain of a failed relationship or job letdown seemed endless, but over time, healing gradually took place. Time allowed me to gain new perspectives, learn valuable lessons, and find the strength I never knew I possessed.

Ecclesiastes 3:1 says, "There is a time for everything, and a season for every activity under the heavens." While time itself does not erase all wounds, it provides us with an opportunity to heal and grow stronger. It gives us space to reflect, process our emotions, and find ways to move forward. It allows us to discover our resilience and the capacity to embrace life again.

As time heals our wounds, it is important to extend ourselves grace and patience. Healing takes time, and it is different for everyone. Embrace your unique pace and grant yourself the space to grieve, heal, and celebrate the little steps of progress along the way.

TIME HEALS

In times of pain, take solace in the understanding that there is a purposeful season for every endeavor. Just as the seasons change, bringing new life and growth, time carries the potential for renewal and transformation in our lives. It is a reminder that the darkest nights eventually give way to the dawn of a new day.

Although we may never forget the pain we have experienced, with time, the sharp edges can become softer, and we can carry on with increased strength and resilience. It teaches us that wounds can become scars, reminding us of our journey and the healing we have experienced.

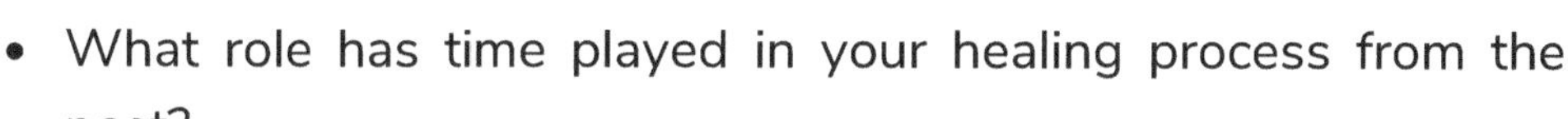

- What role has time played in your healing process from the past?
- Are there any current wounds or struggles in your life that you believe can benefit from the healing power of time? How can you embrace patience and trust in the process of healing?

MAKE PEACE WITH YOUR PAST

Making peace with our past is a transformative journey that opens the door to healing and growth. It requires acknowledging and releasing our burdens, forgiving ourselves and others, and embracing the freedom to live in the present. There may be moments in our lives when we find ourselves trapped by the weight of past mistakes, regrets, or painful experiences. The grip of these memories can hinder our ability to fully embrace the present and step into the future with hope and joy.

I have personally faced the challenge of making peace with my own past. It took time and introspection to recognize the importance of letting go and embracing forgiveness. As I chose to release the pain and resentment, I experienced a newfound sense of liberation and restoration. Isaiah 43:18-19 states, "Forget the former things; do not dwell on the past. See, I am doing a new thing! Now it springs up; do you not perceive it? I am making a way in the wilderness and streams in the wasteland." Through prayer, reflection, and seeking support, we can find the strength to confront our past, make amends where necessary, and forgive ourselves and others.

God promises to make a way in the wilderness and streams in the wasteland. He offers us a fresh start, a new beginning. Letting go of the past allows us to fully embrace the new things He is doing in our lives. It creates space for His transformative work and opens doors to new opportunities and blessings. It is in this process of forgiveness and acceptance that we find healing, wholeness, and the ability to move forward with grace.

Making peace with your past does not mean forgetting or denying its impact on your life. Instead, it is a conscious decision to learn from those experiences, grow stronger, and use them as stepping stones toward a brighter future.

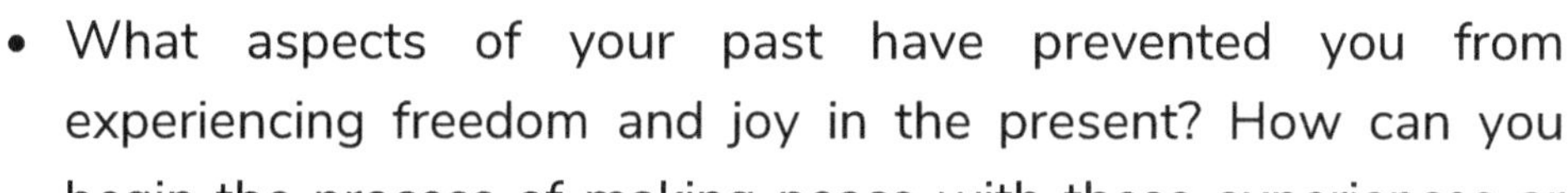

- What aspects of your past have prevented you from experiencing freedom and joy in the present? How can you begin the process of making peace with these experiences or emotions?
- How can you extend forgiveness to yourself and others for past hurts? How might this act of forgiveness contribute to your own healing and growth?

SEEK ABUNDANCE

In a world that often measures success by material wealth and possessions, it's easy to get caught up in pursuing money and the constant chase for more. I, too, found myself on that relentless path, always striving to accumulate more wealth, thinking it would bring me happiness and fulfillment.

I vividly recall a turning point in my life when I shifted my mindset from chasing money to chasing abundance. I came to understand that abundance encompasses more than just monetary riches. It also involves possessing a mindset of appreciation and satisfaction. It is about recognizing and appreciating the blessings that already exist in our lives, regardless of our current circumstances.

Philippians 4:19 states, "And my God will meet all your needs according to the riches of his glory in Christ Jesus." As I began to practice gratitude and focus on the blessings around me, I discovered a newfound sense of joy and fulfillment. I started to appreciate the little things God gives us that often went unnoticed—the sun's warmth on my skin, the laughter of loved ones, and the simple moments of connection. I found abundance in the love and support of family and friends, in the beauty of nature, and in the opportunities for personal growth and self-discovery.

The shift in mindset allowed me to break free from the cycle of chasing external validation and find contentment within myself. It opened my eyes to the countless blessings that were already present in my life, waiting to be acknowledged and cherished.

SEEK ABUNDANCE

Abundance is not measured by the size of your bank accounts but by recognizing the blessings surrounding us. As you embrace the concept of abundance, remember that true wealth is not found in what you possess but in the richness of your experiences, relationships, and inner contentment. Open your heart to the blessings that come your way and choose to live a life of abundance and gratitude.

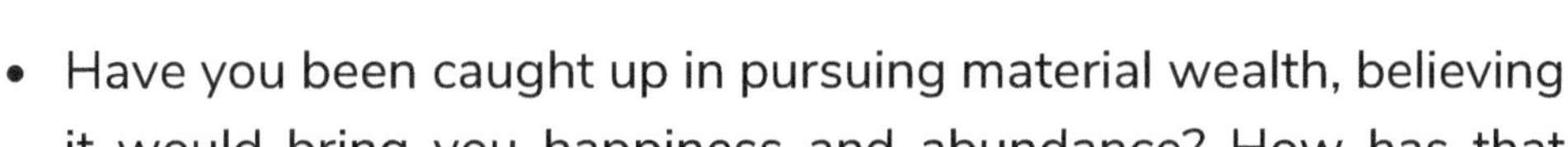

- Have you been caught up in pursuing material wealth, believing it would bring you happiness and abundance? How has that affected your overall sense of joy and fulfillment?
- Consider the blessings that already exist in your life. What are some of the simple joys and moments of abundance that you may have overlooked?

IT'S ON YOU

There was a time in my life when I relied on others to make me happy. I would be sad or disappointed if someone didn't meet my expectations. I have come to understand that genuine happiness cannot be sustained by others; it must originate from within oneself. My happiness is not dependent on others or external circumstances. It is a choice that originates from within me. I hold the power to take control of my thoughts and emotions.

Now, I consciously choose to look for the positives each day. I refuse to allow circumstances to dictate my emotional state. Whether things go as planned or not, I make up my mind to be happy. I refuse to let external factors steal my joy. I often tell myself that regardless of the decisions others make, I will choose to be happy. I'm not going to let the circumstances define my happiness.

Philippians 4:8 says, "Finally, brothers and sisters, whatever is true, whatever is noble, whatever is right, whatever is pure, whatever is lovely, whatever is admirable—if anything is excellent or praiseworthy—think about such things." This scripture reminds us of the importance of cultivating a mindset of gratitude, resilience, and optimism. It means focusing on the things that are true, noble, right, pure, lovely, and admirable. By directing my thoughts toward these positive aspects, I shape my perception and experience of life.

Challenge yourself to break free from the habit of seeking happiness solely from external sources. Instead, nurture a sense of inner contentment and joy that comes from within. Make the deliberate choice to embrace happiness regardless of the circumstances, and watch your outlook transform.

- Recall a recent situation where you allowed external factors to affect your happiness. How did it impact your overall well-being and relationships? What steps can you take to shift your focus towards the positives and regain control of your happiness?
- How can you cultivate gratitude and positivity in your daily life? What practices or habits can you incorporate to train your mind to seek and appreciate the good things around you?

www.ingramcontent.com/pod-product-compliance
Lightning Source LLC
Chambersburg PA
CBHW061143160726
48006CB00038B/2201